Birding through Cancer

A Seasons of Change Journey

Karin Marcus

Seasons of Change® is the registered trademark of Carol McClelland Fields.
Edited by Myra Diaz
Cover by Didona Design. Collage of photographs by Kitty Kono

Balboa Press books may be ordered through booksellers or by contacting:

Balboa Press
A Division of Hay House
1663 Liberty Drive
Bloomington, IN 47403
www.balboapress.com
1 (877) 407-4847

Because of the dynamic nature of the Internet, any web addresses or links contained in this book may have changed since publication and may no longer be valid. The views expressed in this work are solely those of the author and do not necessarily reflect the views of the publisher, and the publisher hereby disclaims any responsibility for them.

Any people depicted in stock imagery provided by Thinkstock are models, and such images are being used for illustrative purposes only.
Certain stock imagery © Thinkstock.

ISBN: 978-1-5043-5654-1 (sc)
ISBN: 978-1-5043-5655-8 (e)

Library of Congress Control Number: 2016906416

Print information available on the last page.

Balboa Press rev. date: 07/18/2016

BALBOA.
PRESS
A DIVISION OF HAY HOUSE

Errata
Page iii – Calligraphy Swan, by Michael Green
Page 53, Line 2 – The Snowy Owl's primary food
source is lemmings not lemurs.
Page 99 – location of photo is John Heinz NWR, PA

Contents

Preparing the Way

A bird does not sing because it has an answer.
It sings because it has a song.
~ Chinese Proverb

That the birds of worry and care fly over your head, this you cannot change,
but that they build nests in your hair, this you can prevent.
~ Chinese Proverb

We cannot know what life has in store for us. Sometimes everything is moving along according to plans and then, dramatically, our life veers off on an unexpected trajectory. Stunned and overwhelmed, with only questions and no answers, we are forced to dig deep. Often we discover hidden strengths that have been quietly developing inside us. These attributes have never before been called upon or tested. Although they cannot necessarily alter events, they may greatly affect how we respond. Miraculously, we discover that all along we have been preparing for this journey.

Little Did I Know

The Elusive Black Rail by Richard Crossley

Nature inspires my everything.
She inspires my solitude, and my writing and my art.
She lifts me upon her welcoming wings
and soars me through the sky of possibilities.
She colors my day, brightens my soul, and calms my nights.
She is fierce and beautiful, strong and delicate — an unrelenting Queen
so generous of advice and never weary of new beginnings.
In spring a colorful maiden, in winter a wise old lady,
in autumn a looking-glass to my falling-leaf self,
and summer a warm blossomed benefactor, comrade to the sun.

~ Terri Guillemets

This is the story of a deeply personal journey through a frightening illness and of eventually regaining a vibrant life. Many have traveled a similar path before me, many will follow, and many others will be their companions along the way.

One of the resounding lessons I have learned is that life often prepares us for the road ahead without our even knowing. Little did I know that my way had already been paved by three core foundations of my life, these being my love for the outdoors, my unique spiritual path, and the intensive, inner personal work involved in becoming a Life Coach.

I begin with my earliest source of comfort and peace, the natural world. As a little girl, I would spend most of my days exploring the welcoming woods behind our home, sitting up in the trees daydreaming, feeling safe in the sheltering arms of their branches. My summer vacations were spent in Cape Cod, Massachusetts, lulled by the perpetual rhythm of the waves as I played in the sand and meandered along the shoreline.

I was quite the spoiled beach snob by the time I moved to Pennsylvania as a young adult. Totally put off by the overcrowded beaches of New Jersey, I rarely saw the ocean except for long family sojourns to my familiar Cape Cod. Many years passed before I finally discovered Cape May Point, New Jersey, where, like much of the outer neck of Cape Cod, here too the beaches are protected by the National Park Service. What a discovery! Instead of the tedious eight-hour drive to the outermost coast of Massachusetts, in just two hours I could be by the ocean, walk the empty beaches and, much to my delight, frequently watch dolphins playing in the surf, the Delaware Bay serving as one of the largest dolphin nurseries on the East Coast.

The discovery of Cape May came at a timely moment in my life. I was a recent empty nester, burnt-out in my work as managing editor of a small publishing company, and at a loss as to what new direction my life was to take. Whenever I needed to clear my head, I would grab my journal and beach chair and retreat to the shore. Once I brought along Barbara Sher's book, *I Could Do Anything If Only I Knew What It Was*, and completed all the exercises while relaxing on the beach. For one exercise, I had to envision the woman I wanted to become. A clear image immediately appeared of me sitting on a porch by the ocean, immersed in conversation with other women. At that time I didn't even know the existence of the Life Coach or Retreat Coach profession. Yet in three years' time, I would be leading women's retreats in Cape May, fulfilling the vision I had seen that day.

It took several visits to Cape May before I finally wandered off the beach and discovered the many other walks available in the area. The South Cape May Meadows Preserve is a serene place to wander amidst low rolling dunes, freshwater wetlands, meadows, ponds, as well as a full mile of protected beach. One day when I was briskly walking the main trail for exercise, I passed two teenage boys in Phillies T-shirts and baseball caps, poised on the ground, their cameras at the ready. An hour later, after completing my loop, they were still there and I inquired what they were doing. "We're waiting for the Black Rail!" they exclaimed, explaining that this was a small bird recently sighted at this location. My curiosity was spiked, and I asked if I could join them. Sure enough, fifteen minutes later this secretive bird scooted across the path and then disappeared into the rushes. The boys' cameras started clicking, and they started jumping up and down, high-fiving one another. They quickly resumed their sitting positions to wait for its return, and twenty minutes later the elusive bird darted back across the path, and the same scene of joy erupted.

Thus began my life as a birder. I did not know then that this was an extremely rare sighting, nor was I able to appreciate that, very likely, never again would I see another Black Rail. Nor did I realize that the South Cape May Meadows Preserve protects over two hundred acres of critical habitat and that Cape May is a globally-renowned birding hot spot. Being a peninsula, Cape May Point creates a migratory funnel and serves as an important resting place before the flight across the broad expanse of the Delaware Bay. It is also a vagrant trap, where many birds never seen in the Northeastern United States come to rest after being blown off course. Little did I know that I too would come to rest in Cape May after being blown way off my life trajectory by cancer. Or that the birding community I found there would be my refuge of sanity throughout the stormy seas of chemotherapy.

Nor did I know that the past decade, during which I had become an established Life Coach and Retreat Coach, had been abundantly providing me with the inner resources to withstand the unforeseen challenges that lay ahead. Once in Mexico, as we were walking through the jungle, a Mayan guide pointed out that for every poisonous plant we passed, within a few feet its remedy could be found growing. Similarly, I've come to understand that, unbeknownst to ourselves, life will gracefully prepare us for what is to come, and that for every challenge, the necessary tools for growth are also within our reach. We just need the eyes to see and the diligence to apply what we discover.

The Sufi Bird

House Sparrow by Adrian Binns

Make a regular practice of telling life what you really want.
You can do this in your journal, as a prayer
before you go to bed, or in conversation with the sky as you walk.
At the end of your request, ask for clear recognizable
signs that you've been heard
and that you will be shown the way.
~ Sara Avant Stover, *The Book of She*

My most heartfelt prayers are frequently released into the universe during long solitary walks in nature. The most repeated prayer is, "God give me strength!" This book is a collection of vignettes relating the solace and guidance I received in answer to that prayer through my many varied encounters along the way.

Most of what I know about prayer comes from my experiences with M.R. Bawa Muhaiyaddeen, a revered Sufi saint from the island of Sri Lanka, who for more than fifty years selflessly shared his wisdom and compassion with people of every race and religion, from all parts of the world. Meeting this sage was by far the most profound encounter of my life.

My husband and I were blessed to live and travel with Bawa Muhaiyaddeen for over twelve years. When asked what it was like to be in the presence of such a mystic, I often relate these two stories.

Solomon and the Sparrow

One day a distraught sparrow came to see Prophet Solomon. "I demand justice!" it implored. "A human destroyed my home and now I have no place to raise my family. This is not right, O Prophet. Please help me!"

"Very well," Solomon replied. "I will look into the matter. Come back tomorrow and I will give you my verdict."

Solomon called the human to appear before him. "I am just the caretaker of the temple," the man humbly pleaded. "This bird built a nest in the rafters, and he was defiling a sacred place with his droppings. I was simply doing my job."

"I will reflect on the matter. Come back tomorrow and I will give you my judgment."

The following day the sparrow and the caretaker appeared before Solomon to hear their fates.

"O sparrow, you are correct. No living being has the right to destroy another's home. And caretaker, you are also correct. It is your duty to keep the temple clean. However, it is just that, if you must destroy one home, you will need to provide this sparrow with another."

And that was when the first birdhouse was built. Humans and birds have been living side by side in harmony ever since.

At first I simply thought that this was just a sweet story that Bawa Muhaiyaddeen would occasionally relate, but later it became a testament to the fact that he truly lived by every word he spoke.

The Sparrow and the Crow

My husband and I had been staying with Bawa for several months in Colombo, Sri Lanka. It was time to return to the ashram in the northern town of Jaffna.

Before dawn, we all piled into a van for the long, hot, bumpy journey. We were tired and headachy when we finally arrived at the ashram eight hours later. When Bawa entered his room to rest, he found that a sparrow had built a nest right behind his bed. In Sri Lanka, pictures rest upon a wooden strip placed a few feet below the ceiling and are angled downward. The bird had built a nest behind a photograph of the Bawa Muhaiyaddeen Fellowship house in Philadelphia.

Immediately Bawa sprang into action. "Bring me some wood and a saw, some nails and a hammer!" And he went to work building a bird house. Once it was complete, it was hung on a pillar of the front balcony. Bawa turned to the sparrow nestled behind the photograph. "This is not a proper place for you to live. I have built you a new home and you should build your nest there." And so it did!

Weeks later, I was sick with dengue fever. I spent endless days lying on my sleeping mat. My only source of entertainment was watching the family of sparrows that lived in the birdhouse outside the window. By now there were two chicks in the nest. Every day I watched the parents dutifully feeding their hungry mouths. The time came for the babies to learn to fly, and the first one boldly took its first solo flight with just a little encouragement. It flew to a nearby window ledge and then back to the birdhouse. The second baby was filled with trepidation. It furiously fluttered its wings only to slip back into the security of the nest. Finally, after the continued insistence of the parents, it took flight and plopped onto the ledge of my open window. Suddenly, startled by someone walking onto the balcony and in fear for its life, the little fledgling again took flight, landing in the rafters above my mat.

For two days, my daytime soap opera continued as I watched the parents trying to encourage this little bird back to the nest. I would awake in the morning to find bird droppings and half eaten bugs on my blanket. Finally on the third day, the little bird found its courage and took a short flight back to the window sill. Again the fledgling was startled by someone entering the room, and out it went. Flying with all its might, it flew past the birdhouse and across the street, onto the roof of the tailor's house.

I jumped up and ran to the window to watch the unfolding drama. The parents were frantic, urging their baby to fly once again and return to the safety of the nest. More secure now in its abilities, the fledgling soon took flight. Just then a big black shadow dove down from the sky above. A crow grabbed the baby in its beak and flew away. The parents dive bombed the crow numerous times, but to no avail. Their baby was gone. I burst into tears and rushed out of my sickroom to tell Bawa the story. He quietly listened and gently consoled me.

That night Bawa was sitting in the main hall where the villagers would come for advice concerning their lives' challenges. The remaining baby bird suddenly appeared on the window ledge by Bawa's shoulder. It started to chirp, "I am all alone in the nest now. It's dark and cold and I'm scared. Can I come in and sleep by you?" Bawa nodded his head in consent and then translated the entire conversation for us.

From that night onward, this little bird would fly into Bawa's room at sunset, sit on the Fellowship photograph above his bed, fluff up its feathers, tuck in its head, and go to sleep.

A picture can express a thousand words, and the image of this little sleeping sparrow perfectly portrayed how it felt to be in the presence of this saint. Its prayers for help had been heard and answered, and it felt protected from the harsh realities of the world.

Since Bawa Muhaiyaddeen's passing in 1986, bereft of his physical presence on which to rely, I have had to seek that refuge of comfort internally, by means of prayer. Still, it always helps to have an outward sign of validation that one's prayers have been heard, and I have come to discover that this is what unexpected encounters in nature can provide for me.

Bawa Muhaiyaddeen once said that if you are ever lost, you can simply walk up to a tree or a stone wall and ask for guidance. The Divine is able to speak through whatever intermediary or language is available. Poets and visionary thinkers have relied upon nature as a source of revelations for centuries. George Washington Carver perfectly expressed it when he said, "I love to think of nature as an unlimited broadcasting station, through which God speaks to us every hour, if we will only tune in."

All of creation, including the human form, consists of the same five elements: earth, fire, water, air and ether. Thus, we are truly coming home when we immerse ourselves in nature. Our connection to the whole is palpable. We are no longer alone in our personal experience but are an integral part of the universal story. This is why we find so many metaphors for life in the natural world. Metaphors form a bridge between our subconscious and conscious awareness. They can be windows into our souls, enabling us to get in touch with our deepest emotions and inner truths.

During my meditational walks, I am mindful of anything unexpected that crosses my path or grabs my attention. Be it a bird, a mammal, a tree, or a rock, I like to pause and reflect upon how it may offer a metaphor for my own life. When I return home, I often look up its totem or symbolic meaning.

Being an avid bird watcher, my eyes are always scanning the trees and the skies. Birds are everywhere, in every habitat, and there are thousands of different species. In all of the major world religions, birds are symbolically associated with the soul, often seen as messengers offering guidance to humans. Carl Jung thought that birds represent the inner spirit of a person and are associated with angels.

The story of "The Sparrow and the Crow" is my first recollection of seeing birds as a metaphor for my innermost heart. This makes it even more befitting that, when faced with the biggest scare of my life, it was birds who became my most frequent messengers of wisdom and who provided ongoing metaphors for my unfolding journey.

It is important to remember that sustainable change is a process. There is no quick fix. Change is a journey, and at the outset you don't know how difficult it might be, how long it may take, or even what your final destination will be. It is also true that your inner season will not always match the outer one. Sometimes this is helpful, sometimes it is not. For example, experiencing the dark winter's night of your soul may be made lighter if it's spring outside, providing a daily reminder of rebirth and renewal. On the other hand, your need to hibernate may be very misunderstood if everyone wants you to come out and play. Nevertheless, understanding what season you are traversing can provide a much needed map to help you find your way.

After years of training with Carol McClelland, I eventually took on the role of training coaches and therapists in the *Seasons of Change* transition modality. In my third year, just after commencing a new semester, the course of my life was suddenly thrown askew by cancer. This was the first major transition I myself had experienced since beginning to train others in this program. Now I desperately needed to apply that knowledge to my own life. Focusing on the tasks of my inner seasons proved profoundly beneficial in calming my fears. During my long *Winter*, I spent a good deal of time journaling, which eventually gave birth to the idea of writing this book. The *Seasons of Change* provided a much needed framework for the many inspirations that birds and the natural world were providing. Just as it enheartened me during a turbulent time, it is my hope that an understanding of this model will provide the reader with the guidance necessary to navigate life's inevitable trials.

The Inner Season of Fall

Autumn asks that we prepare for the future—that we be wise in the ways of garnering and keeping. But it also asks that we learn to let go—to acknowledge the beauty of sparseness.

~ Bonaro W. Overstreet[2]

Fall is a season of dramatic change on the East Coast. The trees are ablaze with reds, oranges, and yellows, all colors traditionally associated with warning signs in our culture. They call us to be attentive, to stop and take heed, slow down and move with caution. Yet often we ignore these warnings and carry on as if life will continue in a habitual fashion.

As soon as we realize that change is coming, we need to prepare for what lies ahead. This preparation may entail examining our options, seeking information, finding support, or creating a refuge. Perhaps the most difficult task for us humans is to control our minds. Fear of the unknown can easily lead us into the bottomless quagmire of "What if this happens, what if that happens?" We become overloaded with the confusion and doubt of endless random possibilities. Remaining focused on the essential tasks of *Fall* helps the mind remain focused on what is actually occurring and necessary in the present moment. It empowers us when we feel most helpless

---

[2]   *Meditations for Women*, (Cokesbury; Abingdon Press 1947). Used by permission. All rights reserved.

Heading South

Full Moon by Kitty Kono

Your life is a sacred journey. And it is about change,
growth, discovery, movement, transformation,
continuously expanding your vision of what is possible,
stretching your soul.
Learning to see clearly and deeply listening to your intuition,
taking courageous challenges at every step along the way.
You are on the path... exactly where you are meant to be right now...
And from here, you can only go forward,
shaping your life story into a magnificent tale of triumph,
of healing, of courage, of beauty, of wisdom, of power,
of dignity, and of love.

~ Caroline Joy Adams

The full moon of the Autumn Equinox was rising on the horizon before me. Normally I would be entranced by the grandeur of its beauty, but today it was a harbinger of the dramatic transition that was just beginning to cast its shadow on my life. I was on the expressway, heading out of Dodge as fast as I could, retreating to a safe haven where I would wait to hear my fate.

Three days prior, I had dutifully gone in for my annual physical examination, during which a mass had been discovered in my abdomen. I was told to get a CAT scan immediately and then speak to an oncologist. That big full moon on the horizon was the "Big C". Cancer. This word holds such power. It looms over you and strikes a fear that pierces your core. Even though intellectually I knew that so many wonderful advances had been made in the treatment of cancer, when I first heard "It might be cancer," instantly I felt as though I had been sentenced to death row and was awaiting the verdict on my appeal.

Unfortunately I was home alone. My husband Carl was away on a business trip, my eldest daughter Halimah lived in Brooklyn and was busily engrossed in her work with the Brooklyn Book Fair, and my younger daughter Noori was out of town visiting friends. She had recently moved back home after getting her Master's degree and was herself tackling difficult heath issues, an outcome of some challenging international field work. So I was on my own, facing an impending undefined threat. Overwhelmed and floundering, I turned to my *Seasons of Change* manual. There was so much I did not yet know, but I understood that this would provide the tools to begin sorting it all out. I now had a survival guide in hand. Feeling like a ship lost at sea that had finally reached a safe harbor, it anchored me.

It was clear that something major was happening which would alter my life from this moment on, but I didn't know the actual diagnosis or the severity of the situation. My immediate task was to not let my mind go wild with possible scenarios and to stay in the present moment with "this much I know for sure." Shock scatters one's *chi*, or life force. I needed space to let the dust settle from this initial explosion. I needed time to assimilate the realization that my life was being propelled into an alternate orbit, destination unknown. Instinctively I knew that I had to retreat into nature.

Another immediate challenge was to adapt to the pace of the medical world: act quickly, wait indefinitely to hear; act quickly, and wait indefinitely. I was told to schedule an immediate CAT scan, which actually posed a wait of several days. Once that was completed, I would have to wait a few more days to hear the results. During this in-between time, I felt utterly disempowered. There was simply nothing to be done. Determined not to sit home alone in nervous anticipation, I drove directly from my CAT scan to my favorite retreat setting, Cape May, New Jersey.

Surprisingly, I couldn't find a single room available anywhere even though it was off season. I finally reserved a tiny room in the top floor of a one hundred and fifty-year-old inn. To get to my room, I had to take a rickety little elevator that needed to be operated by a bell hop. This apparent stepping back in time just added to the surreal aspect of my circumstances. As I settled into my small attic bed, I could see the autumn moon at its pinnacle out my gabled window. I cried myself to sleep, having done all I could for now.

Gathering the Flock

Lift Off by Kitty Kono

Encourage, lift, and strengthen one another.
For the positive energy spread to one will be felt by us all.
For we are connected, one and all.

~ Deborah Day

It was time to focus on another important task of *Fall*—to get my support team in place. This never would have been my initial instinct prior to *Seasons of Change*. One of the common detours of *Fall* is to become a Lone Ranger, and this had certainly been the pattern for much of my life. Since I was a little girl, whenever I was sick I would just go to bed and not get up until I felt better. Assuredly, my old behaviors would not help me now. This was a journey I would not be able to go alone. I also understood from the *Seasons of Change* training that no one person could possibly meet all my needs. It would take a village. This transformative realization was the first of many gifts I received from cancer. I could no longer claim to be self-sufficient and unwaveringly strong. I had to expose my vulnerability, sharing my fears and all my messy emotions, and ask for help.

I saw my team-building as a series of congruent circles. In the center resided those nearest and dearest to my heart, my immediate family. During that initial late night call with my husband, after we had consoled one another, we made a plan to inform Noori once we all got home, and Halimah when her weekend event was over. Telling my daughters proved to be the hardest part of the journey thus far. Their fears were my unspoken fears, their tears were my tears. With Noori, who was presently living at home, we could at least hug and cry and comfort each other. She was so grateful that her own health issues had forced her to move back home, so that she could be there to assist me through the day-to-day challenges. It was harder to tell Halimah in Brooklyn, so I had my husband call and first give her the details of what we knew thus far. Then he handed me the phone, and we just cried. We simply offered one another words of comfort and love.

After the immediate family, I knew I needed my dearest women friends by my side. Girlfriends are incredibly important. As women, we are nurturers of the world, but most of us are hopeless at nurturing ourselves, and that's where girlfriends step in for one another. Research has finally confirmed a truth I've known all along, that time with my women friends is essential to my well being.[4] Best of all they make me laugh through the tears and fears, through my failings

---

[4]   Gale Berkowitz, UCLA Study on "Friendship Among Women: An Alternative to Fight or Flight." ©2002, *Melissa Kaplan's Chronic Neuroimmune Diseases* http://www.anapsid.org/cnd/gender/tendfend.html

and shortcomings. Fortunately, I had several close friends with whom I could open my heart. Knowing me so well, familiar with my inborn reserve at sharing emotions, one dear friend replied, "I'm going to torture you every day with love and attention!" She was true to her word.

The next circle of support included my professional peers. Being a Life Coach, I had several wonderful mentor coaches, people who knew how to bear witness to my process, gently offering encouragement and counsel when needed. First I called Carol McClelland. I was blessed to have in my camp the woman who wrote the book on using nature's wisdom to guide us through changes. I had just begun teaching two new *Seasons of Change* training classes, and Carol generously cleared her schedule and took over the next several weeks of my commitments. Next I reached out to Helene Van Manen, my retreat coach mentor, who had recently been through a similar scenario with a family member. Her soulful listening grounded me. So already I had two top coaches to support and guide me through the months ahead. The third woman was a friend who, inspired by my experience, had decided to also become a Life Coach. Her personal story was one of learning to live with chronic illness and physical pain, and she wanted to share her hard-earned compassion and awareness within her practice. She needed clients so as to accumulate the necessary coaching hours for certification, and I willingly accepted her invitation. These three women became the third tier of my support team.

The fourth circle consisted of people who had professional experience with the situation I was facing, who could help me sort through the onslaught of information and formulate the best decisions. This included two more women friends, one who had recently faced cancer herself, and the other a visiting nurse who had worked within hospice care. As to finding an oncologist, my primary guide here was my gut. I was incredibly thankful to my general practitioner for initially catching the problem, so I chose to not over think this and took a leap of faith, selecting the doctor she was recommending at a local hospital. This turned out to be an excellent choice, particularly when trying to get to the hospital during the rough winter months that lay ahead.

My many-layered support team now in place, the next chore was to decide whom else to tell. There were still family members who needed to be informed, as well as other close friends. This quickly became exhausting. It is very draining to repeat the same story over and over again, to console each person's concerns and worries. Soon it became too much. I relinquished the responsibility and just told all who knew to tell anyone they felt would want to know.

Because this sharing process is so tasking, many people opt to be more private about their predicament. Uncharacteristically for me, this wasn't the case. This decision signified another layer of acknowledging that my life was taking a major shift. It was like putting an open message on my email account, "I will be out of the office for an extended period of time."

Having done all I could for now, it was time to take a big deep breath. Out of curiosity, I looked up the emotional component of this illness in Louise L. Hay's book, *You Can Heal Your Life*. She speaks of illness in the lymph system as "a warning that the mind needs to be re-centered on the essentials of life. Love and joy." I had already instinctively turned to nature for my moments of joy, but an important lesson I still needed to learn was to receive love. I began to see my support team as a flock of Canada Geese flying southward to safe winter grounds, everyone assuming their position to encircle me in a tight formation. They each would take their turn at the lead point, bearing the brunt of the load when needed, then fall to the back and let someone else take the lead. This was love in motion. Surrounded by my flock, I knew I could endure the long journey ahead.

The Barred Owl

Barred Owl by Adrian Binns

Can you be alone without being lonely?
Can you spend time by yourself without
craving noise or company of other people?
Have you discovered the glory of quiet time spent alone,
time spent listening to your soul?
Solitude brings with it gifts that come from nowhere else.

~ Steve Goodier

Throughout this first month of not knowing what lay ahead, my hardest challenge remained to keep my mind under control. I had cleared my schedule because I was incapable of focusing upon other matters at hand. I realized that this newly opened space needed to be replenished by solitary walks in nature. This was my chosen healing meditation that would allow the inner voice of wisdom to be heard.

One morning I awoke feeling anxious. I got dressed and headed out the door yelling to Carl, "I'm going for a walk!" and drove to a local arboretum. After walking for about an hour my anxiety began to seep away, and I found myself in the farthest corner of the property. Suddenly but silently, an owl took flight from its low perch, disappearing deeper into the woods. Although I had gotten but a brief glimpse, I recognized it immediately. I had seen this bird just once before, and it was a memorable experience.

Nearly a year prior to my diagnosis, I was attending a retreat called *Journey Toward Undivided Life,* led by Carol Kortsch and Valerie Brown, at Pendle Hill, a nearby Quaker retreat center. One early morning while the others were in a Quaker meeting for worship, I decided to go for a walk on the nature path that circled the property in order to commune in my favorite chapel, the woods. At the outset of my walk, I posed the question, "Where do I go from here, and how do the varied paths my life has taken merge into one undivided purpose?"

Amidst the young forest was a spattering of ancient trees. I stopped to stand beneath a one hundred and fifty-year-old giant beech, sensing the history of all that this tree had witnessed and how every broken branch and scar marring its bark, etched both by humans and the elements, bore witness to its durability, resiliency, and steadfastness. Pensively walking on, the path led me through a silent copse of evergreens where I was welcomed by its stillness and coolness. As I came around the next bend, something flew down the path ahead of me. I quietly followed and there, waiting for me around the next turn, was a Barred Owl sitting low on a branch. We momentarily gazed into each other's eyes and then it took off and continued down the path. I followed, and again it was waiting for me around the next bend; again we silently took each other in. This pattern repeated itself two more times, until on the fourth occasion the owl veered off and vanished into the woods, as if to say, "Okay, enough. I think you got the point."

As I stood there, I experienced a deep knowing that I was on the right path, and that my spiritual teacher was always present and guiding me. When needed, he would appear to reassure me. All that was required of me was to keep placing one foot in front of the other, and the way would become clear.

The owl is a symbol of the sacred feminine, of prophecy and wisdom. On one of the many totem websites, I read that this totem can teach you to use your voice with greater effect, to trust your instincts about people, and to hear not only what is being said but also what is hidden. That is an astute description of active listening, one of the core competencies for a Life Coach.

I had come to this retreat seeking to incorporate, more deeply into my work, the profound experience of having studied with a Sufi Master. To be able to professionally integrate this most definitive aspect of my life signified the undivided life I was seeking. The encounter with the owl revitalized my resolution to place my teacher in front of me and listen, first within my own life and then through the callings of my work. It also inspired a simple practice that I would come to follow in order to invite divine wisdom into every coaching session. I would silently begin with a simple prayer:

> May what needs to be said, be said.
> May what needs to be heard, be heard.
> May what needs to be understood, be understood.

My only duty now was to keep my heart open to hear the responses.

Somewhere along the way, I also realized that leading an undivided life does not mean that my inner and outer lives need to merge as one, identically the same. This actually can be very unwise. There are too many harsh forces in this world completely beyond one's control, and the sacred innermost heart must be treasured and protected. Living an undivided life does mean, however, that my inner and outer lives must be in harmony. This is not a static, achieved state. Rather, it is a perpetually shifting balancing act, a constant dance with each partner always being aware of the other's moods and movements—allowing the vulnerable, tender, gentle self to lead whenever the music so dictates and then giving way to the strong, determined, protective side as the tempo changes. Those mystical moments do exist when one is standing amidst a vortex and both worlds coexist in perfect harmony. I am reminded of once watching a performance by the eminent Russian ballet star, Rudolph Nureyev. He would launch into the air with a magnificent leap and when he reached the pinnacle he seemed to stop, remaining perfectly still. Frozen. Aloft. Then, without skipping a beat, the dance would resume.

This encounter with the owl was a similarly heart-stopping moment. It showed me that I only needed to unflinchingly proceed forward, without the ballast of fear or doubt. Ironically, several weeks later one of my clients introduced me as her "spiritual coach," a title I would never dare to assume. Apparently unbeknown to me, I already was doing what I was striving to become. By focusing on living an undivided life and attending to my own inner life, my personal growth was naturally and effortlessly being reflected in my work.

Now a year later at the arboretum, the Barred Owl had showed itself, for the second time in my life, to remind me I was not alone, and more importantly, that if throughout this illness I remained focused on my inner state, the benefit would be reflected in my physical health. A world-renowned expert on women's health and a maverick in her field, Christiane Northrup, M.D. stresses this point in her book *Goddesses Never Age*:

> *The most important thing you need to know about your health is that the health of your body and its organs does not exist separate from your emotional well-being, your thoughts, your cultural programming, and your spiritual outlook. Your thoughts and beliefs are the single most important indicator of your health.*

My undivided approach to my cancer must be to follow the medical recommendations of my doctor while mindfully nurturing my innermost well-being.

While I was out looking for solace in the woods, my husband was at home meditating. He too was seeking guidance for his own worried heart. After sharing my experience of the encounter with the owl, he told me that he too had received a similar clear message, that this was going to be an arduous journey, but everything would be okay. In our own ways, we both had found the reassurance we needed.

I am beginning to see a pattern. Whenever I have an intuitive glimpse at a deeper understanding, the same message is conveyed through another source. The universe keeps reinforcing its messages, just in case I'm doubtful or forgetful or thick-headed. After all, it knows I'm only human.

Riding the Thermals

Broad-winged Hawk by Richard Crossley

Inner resources are what we find when we are called upon
to cope with what we cannot control.
~ Suzanne Braun Levine, *Inventing the Rest of Our Lives*

Carl and I were to meet with my oncologist and finally get more definitive results. The previous night I had once again plummeted into the dual emotional woes of not knowing and fear of what I might learn. Stepping out onto my front porch that morning, I saw six Broad-winged Hawks circling above. These hawks often migrate in large kettles of hundreds or even thousands, but this was the first time I had ever seen even one in my neighborhood, so six was very exciting. They were effortlessly circling, riding the warm, rising air of the thermal currents. By flying in a spiraling circular path within these columns, birds are able to ascend to higher altitudes while expending very little energy in the process.

According to Native American cultures, hawks appear in our lives when we need to pay attention to subtle messages and underlying truths. Hawks gracefully and effortlessly glide between the seen and unseen realms, connecting both together. When researching the hawk totem, one particular passage struck me:

> *The destiny of all mankind is to awaken from their spiritual amnesia and realign with the original intention of their soul. When a hawk flies into our life, we will be asked to evaluate who we have become and rip out the threads of our self-created illusions. This enables our inner truth to surface.*[5]

Wake up! More is happening here than a mere physical ailment. Shaken by the unexpected, I had let fear rush in. Like the Broad-winged Hawk riding the thermals, I needed to channel that energy into a rising surge that would elevate me to a higher level of understanding.

Preparing to hear my fate and move from the realm of not knowing to knowing necessitated transforming my fear into faith. Not the belief that all would be magically fixed, but the deep knowing that, along with the challenges, I would be given the guidance to manage the journey. Such faith doesn't require a specific outcome, but trusts that the necessary lessons will be learned.

---

[5] Ina Woolcott, "Hawk Power Animal Messenger Discernment Intuition Observation Wisdom Courage Truth", *Shamanic Journey,* 2015. http://www.shamanicjourney.com/ hawk-power-animal-messenger-discernment-intuition-observation-wisdom-courage-truth

Having fallen into an abyss with my initial diagnosis, I now needed to affirm that although I could not control the narrative of my life and write the "perfect" script, I could determine how I would ride the storm.

Sure enough, as the hawks' presence heralded, things were beginning to look up. When we finally had our first meeting with my oncologist, he did a lot to calm my fears. More tests were needed, but he felt hopeful that this wasn't going to be a drastic scenario. I felt a little lighter and more able to gently ride the winds of the seemingly eternal waiting game.

Hope

Northern Waterthrush by Adrian Binns

Hope is the thing with feathers
That perches in the soul
And sings the tune without the words
And never stops at all.

~ Emily Dickinson

Halimah came down from New York to be supportive. This was the first time we had seen each other since she had been delivered the distressing news over the phone, and we both needed a hug. For our mother-daughter bonding time we spent the afternoon at one of my favorite local birding spots, the John Heinz National Wildlife Refuge. Surrounded by Interstate 95, the Philadelphia airport, gas tankards, and low-income housing, this freshwater tidal marsh was America's first urban refuge, established in 1972. There are miles of trails that wander through woodlands along a tidal river and encircle a large area of open water and mudflats. This is truly a sanctuary, a consecrated place where life is protected, supporting hundreds of species that rest here during migration, or that call it home year-round.

While Halimah jogged around the perimeter, I had time for a short walk to see what birds might be about. Soon I spotted a Northern Waterthrush at the water's edge, foraging in the mud. Although guides had pointed this bird out to me before, this was the first time I identified one by myself. A small simple victory on a lovely day.

In Diane Wells' book, *100 Birds and How They Got Their Names,* she quotes Thomas Hardy's description of the thrush's song: "Hope whereof he knew/ And I was unaware." Hope? Yes, we're all hoping for a positive outcome, but I was also preparing myself to deal with whatever reality unfolded. It's a balancing act, maintaining hope for the future while remaining grounded in whatever each day presents. The presence of this Waterthrush was reminding me that whatever the future might bring, hope sings on.

In this uplifted frame of mind, a few days later I headed off for my next test, which was a biopsy. Even though this was to be a minor out-patient procedure, it was nonetheless very nerve-wracking. I have never understood why hospital waiting rooms find it necessary to have the television blaring. This day the CNN news was blasting something in the usual manner of, "Stay tuned to hear the latest life-threatening situation you must know about immediately!" Just what patients and loved ones need to hear. At least on airplanes they do it right, showing calm videos of waterfalls in a forest, prior to taking off. I find it such a relief in my ophthalmologist's office that she only shows National Geographic specials.

In order to manage my stress and vulnerability, I was being very protective with regard to what I was reading, as well as the movies and television shows that I watched. So I came to this visit prepared with earplugs to block out the annoying television and toting a nice uplifting book, *What I Know Now: Letters to My Younger Self* by Ellyn Spragins. This is a collection of letters written by famous women, who share acquired wisdom they now possess and wish they had known when they were younger. I read two lovely chapters by Maya Angelou and Madeline Albright, and then I turned to one written by Queen Noor of Jordan. There in her preface, she shares that her husband, King Hussein, died of non-Hodgkin's Lymphoma! Immediately my mind screamed, "Oh my God, that's what I have—and he had the best doctors in the world!" Despite all the protective boundaries I had put in place, negativity still managed to slither in. I slammed the book closed in an attempt to shut my mind to those thoughts. That's when they called my name to come in for the procedure.

I needed to still my pounding heart. While being prepped, awaiting blood test results, and finally during the procedure itself, I just kept focusing on my breath, intentionally breathing in all that is healing and pure, exhaling all that is negative and depleting; breathing in hope, exhaling worry. A few times they stopped to check whether I was okay, because I was so quiet and still. Afterward, as the nurse wheeled me out of the hospital, she asked, "How do you remain so calm?"

"I just pray," I replied.

The next day I had my final test, a PET scan. After three more endless days of waiting, I met with my oncologist for the results. While I had Stage Three non-Hodgkin's Lymphoma, it was only Grade Two, which meant that it was the very slow-growing, non-aggressive type. Not the type King Hussein had endured, the doctor assured me! This was very good news. It meant that I would require only six months of chemotherapy entailing two consecutive days of treatment once a month. A huge weight lifted from my heart. For the first time I felt, "I can do this!" It echoed the answer Carl had received in his meditation. This would be difficult, but manageable.

Looking back, those weeks of waiting had comprised the most difficult times of my entire treatment. The not knowing is an agonizing cancer of the mind and heart. Finally I had been given some answers and now knew what to prepare for. My next *Fall* task would be to ready my nest so I could settle into a long *Winter* of six months.

The Inner Season of Winter

Nature looks dead in winter because her life is gathered into her heart.
She withers the plant down to the root
that she may grow it up again fairer and stronger.
She calls her family together within her inmost home
to prepare them for being scattered abroad
upon the face of the earth.

~ Hugh Macmillan

Winter is a time of both hardship and beauty. Days are shorter, the air is crisper. Nature becomes a study in black and white, with snow-covered ground accentuating the stark outline of naked trees. The scarcity of resources forces plants to become dormant and animals to migrate or hibernate. All life forms slow down and find ways to adapt to the harsh environment. Likewise, we humans wrap ourselves in protective clothing and hunker down in warm, comforting shelters.

Inwardly, *Winter* is the "dark night of our soul", when we feel lost, aimlessly wandering as we strive to find our bearings. The dramatic change from abundance to scarcity can be exhausting, physically, emotionally, and spiritually. We need to protect ourselves during this vulnerable time, to rest and renew on all levels. Not knowing how long or how severe our *Winter* will be, we must diligently conserve our precious energy and resources. *Winter* is the time to reconnect with our core being, the essence of who we are beyond our roles and responsibilities. It is a time to surrender to "not knowing" and just focus on the next step in front of us until our new path is revealed.

My Cocoon

Monarch Butterfly by Kitty Kono

The winter solstice has always been special to me
as a barren darkness that gives birth to
a verdant future beyond imagination,
a time of pain and withdrawal that produces
something joyfully inconceivable, like a monarch butterfly
masterfully extracting itself from the confines of its cocoon,
bursting forth into unexpected glory.

~ Gary Zukav[6]

The initial roller coaster ride had cruised to a stop. The doctor said that I would not be drastically nauseous, that after each treatment my immune system would remain low for about ten days, but then it would start to build up again. I would not be completely debilitated and could continue teaching, coaching, and exercising. In fact, he encouraged me to do so.

Best of all, he also said that I would not lose my hair, although it might thin a bit. This to me was a really big deal. In recent years, it has become a badge of selfless courage for friends and family members to shave their heads as a stand of solidarity with loved ones facing this ordeal. To my mind, losing my hair would have been the equivalent of announcing to the world, "I have cancer!" It wasn't a matter of vanity, but an invasion of privacy, exposing my naked vulnerability. Looking back, I can see that this was a decisive motivating factor in my telling so many people, so early on, what I thought soon would be apparent for all to see.

People sometimes inquired whether I had experienced any premonition at all that something was wrong, and it has occurred to me that in the weeks prior to my diagnosis, wherever I went I was noticing women wearing scarves or hats covering their bald heads. I remember thinking this to be unusually prevalent, and I simply gave each woman a warm smile in passing. It did evoke in me the thought, "There but by the grace of God go I." I now knew that this side effect of hair loss was not to be one of my struggles, although I would share many others with this new sisterhood.

My first chemo appointment was scheduled within just a few weeks. I needed to prepare myself physically, mentally, and emotionally for this rapidly-approaching season. Nature slows down in winter; animals instinctively know they need to conserve their energy during these

---

6   Gary Zukav, http://seatofthesoul.com/2011/12/solstice-joy/

taxing months. My body was going to undergo a chemical attack, and similarly I needed to seek protective shelter. I needed to create a cocoon where I could rest through my *Winter* until I was ready to re-emerge in the *Spring*, hopefully transformed by all that I would experience.

It was crucial to find the right balance and be very selective as to how I used my time. From Cheryl Richardson's book *The Art of Extreme Self-Care,* one line became my motto: "If it's not an absolute YES, it's a NO!" And another valuable nugget of advice: "The most powerful way we can create a soul-loving space is to simply remove fifty percent of what's there." She was talking about physical space, but I applied it to my emotional environment. This meant that I had to say NO to a wonderful opportunity to give a *Seasons of Change* presentation to the local chapter of the International Coaching Federation. I also had to step away from a major divisive issue that was engulfing a spiritual community very dear to my heart. Instead of exercising four times a week, I reduced it to two.

I said YES to those activities that I felt would truly deepen my personal journey. At this point I had no idea how I would be feeling, but I completely emptied my calendar for the weeks that I was scheduled for chemo. For the rest of each month, I chose to continue with my one-on-one coaching practice. This would serve to give me a sense of purpose and actually enhance my energy level. It also felt relevant to continue the *Seasons of Change* training classes and share my situation with the students, allowing them to benefit from the real-time experience of observing this transition model being applied during a health crisis. At the same time, it would help me maintain my focus on the seasonal tasks at hand.

I also continued my women's support group, which had been meeting weekly for several years. A great deal of trust had developed among these women, and the sharing was a great source of learning for myself as well. For example, we were reading and discussing *Kitchen Table Wisdom* by Rachel Naomi Remen, M.D. Given my circumstances, one particular chapter, *Embracing Life,* particularly resonated with me. It talked about "the power of taking an unconditional approach to life … a willingness to show up for whatever life may offer and meet with it, rather than wishing to edit and change the inevitable."

An unconditional acceptance of life: What a powerful concept! We all have a deep-felt need for unconditional love, but it is an ideal rarely fulfilled, perhaps because we've missed a vital pre-requisite—the unconditional acceptance of life. This concept embraces the belief that everything happens for a reason or, more accurately, there is something to be learned from every situation. Its realization silences all the self-doubts and self-criticisms, senseless blaming, and the endless lamenting of "Why me?" It opens the door to self-love, a threshold that is necessary to cross before one can unconditionally love another.

Part of me, deep down inside, innately knew this truth. This wiser Self knew that, in reality, the unexpected twists and valleys of life often provide the most profoundly transformative experiences. Perhaps this is because frequently when we are the most challenged and vulnerable, the true beauty of our humanity is illuminated. The following story served as an excellent reminder of this understanding as I prepared to enter my *Winter*.

The Butterfly Story

A man found a cocoon of a butterfly. One day a small opening appeared. He sat and watched the butterfly for several hours as it struggled to force its body through that little hole. Then it seemed to stop making any progress. It appeared as if it had gotten as far as it could and could go no farther.

So the man decided to help the butterfly. He took a pair of scissors and snipped off the remaining bit of the cocoon. The butterfly then emerged easily. But it had a swollen body and small, shriveled wings.

The man continued to watch the butterfly because he expected that at any moment the wings would enlarge and expand to be able to support the body, which would itself contract in time. Neither happened! In fact the butterfly spent the rest of its life crawling around with a swollen body and shriveled wings. It was never able to fly.

What the man in his kindness and haste did not understand was that the restricting cocoon and the struggle required for the butterfly to get through the tiny opening were nature's way of forcing fluid from the body of the butterfly into its wings, so that it would be ready for flight once it achieved its freedom from the cocoon.

Sometimes struggles are exactly what we need in our life. If we went through our life without any obstacles, it would cripple us. We would not be as strong as what we could have been. And we could never fly.

So have a nice day and struggle a little. When you're under pressure and stress, remember that you are a better person after you have gone through it.[7]

Like the emerging butterfly, I had to go through this difficult period, and yet already I had received a glimpse of the tremendous grace and personal growth that could result from this challenging journey. Having no control over the outcome, all I could do was to show up and give it my best.

My wise Self knew that an unconditional acceptance of life is not a passive stance. Rather, it is the highest form of proactive living. Without judgment, I needed to meet each circumstance with unreserved curiosity. "What must I learn from this? What are the hidden gifts to be discovered? What are the possibilities? How will this stretch my soul?" The ultimate goal would be to refine this understanding into a day-to-day, moment-by-moment attitude toward life.

This state of acceptance would allow me to be fully present and vibrantly alive. As Rachel Naomi Remen further explains, it actually is the true source of joy.

Joy seems to be a part of an unconditional wish to live, not holding back because life might not meet our preferences and expectations. Joy seems to be a willingness to accept the whole, and to show up and meet whatever is there. It is a kind of invincibility that attachment to any particular outcome would deny us.

---

[7] Paulo Coelho, Adapted from a story by Sonaira D'Avila, http://paulocoelhoblog.com/2007/12/10/the-lesson-of-the-butterfly/

Your problem is how you are going to spend
this one odd and precious life you have been issued.
Whether you're going to spend it trying to look good
and creating the illusion that you have power
over people and circumstances,
or whether you are going to taste it,
enjoy it and find out the truth about who you are.

~ Anne Lamott[8]

"It's my birthday, and I got cancer!" No matter how much I tried to remain focused on the positive, at the slightest opening, the negative gremlins were ready to pounce. Bawa Muhaiyaddeen was once asked, "When will I ever be able to overcome my monkey-mind and stop its endless chatter?"

"Never," he replied, "That's just what the monkey-mind does and will always do. But one day, you may learn to stop listening and reacting to it."

On other occasions, he also advised that one of the best ways to silence the monkey-mind is to distract it. For example, give a monkey a mirror and he will be enamored for hours. What better mirror is there than nature?

By now it was evident that this was going to be a long journey, and it would be an ongoing challenge to sustain the quality of mindfulness throughout an extended *Winter*. Silencing the monkey-mind would require more extensive opportunities for reflection than my occasional sojourns into the woods. I needed a bigger mirror.

Right on cue, the perfect invitation arrived in my email box:

Join a circle of wise women for a soulful year-long adventure. Immerse yourself in deep healing conversation—with yourself, each other, and the beautiful land, sky, and water of this country. Come with your pressing questions, your silence, your open heart, your deep listening, and a spirit of joyful adventure, knowing that we

---

8   Anne Lamott, Commencement Speech at University of California at Berkeley, 2003 http://www. graduationwisdom.com/speeches/0043-lamott.htm

will each find what our souls need, and that the seeds planted together can keep growing into action and service in the days ahead.

The invitation was from Carol Kortsch, who had led that wonderful retreat at Pendle Hill where I encountered the Barred Owl. Her new offering, *Sustaining Your Wild and Precious LIFE! A Year-Long Pilgrimage of Soul in a Circle of Women,* included four mini-retreats at her home and a closing weekend in the Appalachian Mountains. Conveniently dovetailing with all the medical appointments, I now had these bi-monthly appointments to check in with my soul and to monitor my progress on the inward journey.

The initial gathering was scheduled for two weeks after my first chemo, which did not go as smoothly as had been anticipated. It totally knocked the stuffing out of me. I experienced the classic chemo nightmare of bowing to the porcelain god, sick as a dog, with a raging headache. I felt extremely weak and emotionally deflated. My worst fears seemed to be coming true—that this was going to be an arduous, drawn-out test of endurance.

When I arrived at Carol's, I felt wobbly. It literally seemed as if the ground beneath my feet was unstable, as though I had experienced an earthquake. I had lost my footing, but once again the stars aligned; the theme for the day's retreat was *Earth-Grounding Roots.*

After a few lovely hours sitting by the fire, conversing and reading poetry about trees and our sustaining Earth Mother, I was already feeling more grounded and stabilized. Next we were sent off for some solitary time to reflect and journal. Entering the woods, I found a tree with large exposed surface roots extending outward in many directions. One particularly smooth and wide root provided a very comfortable seat, with the tree's strong straight trunk supporting my back. I reflected that this mighty presence did not obtain its strength and longevity from the roots upon which I rested, but from its unseen taproot and heartwood.

The taproot is a strong primary root that grows very deep, vertically straight downward. Webster's Dictionary further defines it as "the central element or position in a line of growth or development." Sitting beneath its protective presence, this tree gently reminded me that the taproot of faith must serve as my central support and focus in order to sustain my growth throughout the current challenges. This was the anchor that would hold me upright. I had weathered the first storm of chemo, and I was still standing.

The trunk of a tree, such as the one that was providing my back with much-needed support, gains its strength from the heartwood. This central core of the tree is as strong as steel; a board

The Inner Season
of Summer

Rest is not idleness, and to lie sometimes on the grass
on a summer day listening to the murmur of water,
or watching the clouds float across the sky,
is hardly a waste of time.

~ John Lubbock

It's time to celebrate. We have completed a long arduous journey and it is important to fully acknowledge our accomplishments. Take a deep breath. Savor the fresh air and open space. Like a child just released from the concrete confines of school, frolic in the joys of summer! It's time to play and to relish our newfound freedom.

Life is at its most abundant, and we need to allow the fruits of our labors to ripen. A burdensome weight has been lifted from our hearts and there is a joyful lightness to our spirits. We have a new sense of clarity, confidence, and empowerment. Life is good. It is important to fully appreciate life's rich bounty. *Summer* is precious, and all too fleeting.

Released into the Wild

Puerto Rican Parrot with Tracking Collar by Carl Marcus

To nurture a soulful, creative life that is of benefit to others,
we need to reconnect tenderly with our wild soul.
We need to create a loving, open, non-judgmental
space for our tender parts to gain footing and courage.
We need to create a clear path for the flow of Spirit through our lives.
~Annie O'Shaughnessy

I'm done with chemo! What an incredible feeling of relief. To celebrate, we had a family dinner at a very chic farm-to-table restaurant in Philadelphia. When it was time for a toast, I felt it important to thank each member of my family personally for the support they had given me over the past months. Tears freely flowing, I struggled to voice my heartfelt words. I thanked Carl for being my rock, for his confident assurance that we would get through this; Noori for being my daily companion, bringing a sense of humor and laughter into my difficult days; and Halimah, my weekend visitor and chef, who filled up the fridge with delicious, soothing soups. The silver lining of this illness was the strengthening of our family bond and the impetus to fully express our love for one another. For that I will be forever grateful. Together we savored every bit of this extravagant meal, nourished beyond expectations.

To continue the celebration, Carl and I went on a birding trip to Puerto Rico. Carl is often a willing companion on my short birding treks, enjoying the outdoors and his photography, but he isn't as avid a birder and wasn't sure if he would enjoy five full days of birding. So this trip was truly his gift to me.

Gabriel, our *Wildside Nature Tours* guide, picked us up at the San Juan airport and off we went, a merry band of eight bird enthusiasts. Over the next several days we would circle the island, birding from dawn to dusk. A few evenings we even reconvened after dinner and went on night walks, looking for the Puerto Rican Screech Owl. It felt exotic to walk in the dark forest surrounded by an army of frogs creating an endless cacophonic symphony. We traveled the back roads and stayed far away from the tourist hot spots. At most of the state forests we visited, we were the only people there.

Puerto Rico has eighteen endemics, birds that exist solely on this island, and we managed to see seventeen of them, only missing one, though hearing the elusive Screech Owl. Our most exciting sighting was the Puerto Rican Parrot. A mere one hundred are still in existence in the wild and four hundred in captivity. We traveled to the Río Abajo State Forest where, as part of a recovery program, captive-reared parrots are being released into the wild. After hiking to an area they were known to inhabit, we stood for over an hour before we finally heard one calling. Even then it took another hour to actually spot one. Finding a green parrot in a green jungle isn't easy.

What a celebration of life to see this endangered species slowly making a comeback through the dedicated efforts of a handful of people. I also felt that I had been released back into the wild, freed from the confines of the cancer center where I too had been cared for by a dedicated staff. It was an overwhelming relief to have the chemo behind me. No longer would I have to sit for endless hours in the sole chair that had a view of the outside world. I truly felt like a caged bird that had been set free. It was exhilarating to be flying again.

In her book *Refuge: An Unnatural History of Family and Place*, Terry Tempest Williams shares some of her mother's story of battling breast cancer. After recuperating from two major operations, chemotherapy, and radiation, she and her husband went on a trip to Switzerland. In a letter to Terry she wrote, "More and more, I am realizing the natural world is my connection to myself. Landscape brings me simplicity. I can shed the multiplicity of things at home and take one duffle bag wherever I go."[16] This beautifully mirrored my experience. On this trip I was able to shed the heavy baggage of the deeply insidious fear that had been weighing me down, gradually allowing my wild soul to reawaken.

Equally poignant, she added, "The natural world is a third party in our marriage. It holds us close and lets us revel in the intimacy of all that is real." However lonely it may have felt at times, my illness has been our shared experience, and going on this adventure with Carl was essential to our mutual healing process. The added gift of the trip was recognizing how deeply our love of nature unites us. Hiking and enjoying the outdoors had been a large part of our courtship and early years together. Now forty years later, it was a timely reminder to return to our shared love of the natural world.

---

[16]   Terry Tempest Williams, *Refuge: An Unnatural History of Family and Place,* (New York, Vintage Books, 2001), 86-87.

Returning to Fall

History doesn't repeat itself, but it often rhymes.
~ Mark Twain

Having completed the cycle of the seasons, having weathered the dark night of the soul, emerging stronger and more fully authentic, it is time once again to embrace the rhythm of transformation. Summer is all too brief, and autumn is always right on its heels, but now we find welcoming comfort in the natural order of things. It's like a familiar refrain, but with new orchestration.

In this new cycle of seasons, it is helpful to recognize the early signs of *Fall* and to observe as they gradually, sequentially appear. This gives us time to prepare both emotionally and physically, allowing for a gentler transition. As with every *Fall*, the tasks are the same—examining our options, seeking information, finding support, and creating a refuge. However these endeavors are familiar friends now and it feels good to welcome them back.

Spring Migration in *Fall*

Blue-headed Vireo by Adrian Binns

Your living is determined not so much by what life brings to you
as by the attitude you bring to life;
not so much by what happens to you
as by the way your mind looks at what happens.

~ Khalil Gibran

With fortuitous timing, my next retreat with Carol Kortsch was scheduled for the day after I received the news that I would need further treatments. This would be a comforting refuge in which to continue processing this new predicament. Carol has created an elaborate garden sanctuary in her own backyard, brimming with both exotic and indigenous plants, a small trickling waterfall and lily pond, as well as a stream meandering through a forested area.

With many inviting little nooks to sit and be contemplative, I chose a serene spot in the woods by the stream. Soon, some of the early spring migrants began to join me—a Black and White Warbler, a Ruby-crowned Kinglet, and a Blue-headed Vireo. Eight months before, when I had embarked on this journey, the birds had been heading south, and now they were returning north to their breeding grounds. The eternal cycle of the seasons continues unbroken.

My lymphoma journey was changing direction as well. I was re-entering the season of *Fall*. Sitting by the stream, it occurred to me that if I did proceed with this maintenance plan, having treatments every other month for two years would only amount to twelve days! And even counting the CAT scans every six months added up to a mere total of sixteen days out of seven-hundred and eighty-four! That seemed totally doable. This second cycle through my inner *Seasons of Change* was promising to be a lot smoother and easier.

Once again I needed to focus upon the tasks of *Fall* by updating my support team and formulating decisions toward subsequent steps. My immediate challenge was to decide whether or not to follow the advice of my oncologist and proceed with the maintenance plan. Initially my intention had been that the completion of chemotherapy would culminate my tour of Western medicine, whereupon I would turn to Eastern medicine to restore my health. Should I keep with that plan or revamp it? I needed to hear the opinions of my support team. After discussing the situation with my naturopath, acupuncturist, and friends with experience in this arena, I conveyed all the information to my husband. After praying on the matter, we sat down with our daughters and together we made a unified decision as how to move forward. Everyone agreed that I would pursue every option available, both Eastern and Western.

Eight months prior, in my panic and distress, I had made all sorts of promises to God: to pray more, to be of more service, to clean up my act and eliminate the duality of what was felt and expressed in my inner world from what I manifested in my outer life. Like New Year's resolutions, these promises had lost their momentum. God was keeping his side of the bargain and had granted me a manageable challenge, but I was forgetting my part of the deal. God is used to that, I think.

The hidden gift of my maintenance plan was that it also served as a recurring reminder of my promises. I had much more yet to accomplish in this lifetime: I still needed to blossom more fully, to become the person I was created to be. I saw this new arrangement as a periodic kick in the butt to keep up my end of the bargain. With this attitude shift, I also realized that this cancer was no longer the driving force in my life. It had taken a backseat. My job would be to not allow it to become a backseat driver.

Again it came back to silencing the monkey-mind. I am reminded of this often-told Cherokee tale:

> *An old Cherokee was teaching his grandson about life. "A fight is going on inside me," he said to the boy.*
>
> *"It is a terrible fight, and it is between two wolves. One is evil—he is anger, envy, sorrow, regret, greed, arrogance, self-pity, guilt, resentment, inferiority, lies, false pride, superiority, and ego." He continued, "The other is good—he is joy, peace, love, hope, serenity, humility, kindness, benevolence, empathy, generosity, truth, compassion, and faith. The same fight is going on inside you—and inside every other person too."*
>
> *The grandson thought about it for a minute and then asked his grandfather, "Which wolf will win?"*
>
> *The old Cherokee simply replied, "The one you feed."* [17]

---

[17] "Two Wolves: A Cherokee Legend", *The First People*,
http://www.firstpeople.us/FP-Html-Legends/TwoWolves-Cherokee.html

Recently, I had doubted the value of writing this book, questioning who the audience might be. My only answer thus far had been that I needed to write this for myself, so as to understand my own journey. Here amongst this grove of trees, it felt as if I was being encouraged to speak, to be an open book, that there might be a few who needed to hear my story.

Placing the frame upon the stone, I observed that this rock was a conglomerate of many small pebbles held together by minute sparkling grains of sand. My story isn't just this illness; it is, I realized, a conglomeration of all that lead up to it. All that Bawa Muhaiyaddeen had taught me, all the therapy, coaching, training, and personal work I had done had all served to shape a fertile soul, ready to be cracked open and revealed.

It was time to return to the group. I took a path around a lake, one that I had walked numerous times before. There at the beginning of the path was a bright red fall leaf. But it was July! As if heralding the beginning of my new inner *Fall*, it signified that I had completed the initial cycle of my journey and another was to follow. A few steps further, I encountered a pile of black feathers and white down, the remains of a crow. A dead crow is a symbol of good fortune, the death of something ominous. Like cancer?

This day had been filled with many illuminating moments. However, I have learned that these experiences will simply dissipate into the ethers if not followed up by action. I was filled with a new resolve to complete this book, to keep that remembrance flowing thorough my soul.

My Egg by Karin

Independence Day

Fledgling Carolina Wren by Kitty Kono

Who can see inside the deepest recesses of your imagination and manifest those wishes
into your daily experience? Who can appreciate those subtle nuances of character you've
acquired by overcoming your deepest fears? Who can truly respect those things
that are no longer a part of you because of all your work to release them?
Who can see the strength left behind in the wake of your unique struggles and
obstacles? Who will see you for who you are, appreciating everything that is there,
everything that is not, everything that can be, if you do not? Who else can?

~ Vironika Tugaleva

My primary focus now was to regain my vitality. I still needed to be protective of my time and keep my calendar free of unnecessary burdens. It was time to walk the talk again. I once created a personal energy grid for one of my retreats called Soular Power. It included a worksheet for recording all one's energy drainers and energy enhancers. For our lives to prosper, the input of positive energy needs, at the very least, to be in balance with our output, a state of equanimity between what we receive and what we give. Ideally, the input should be even greater, so that we can establish a reserve for times of unexpected stress and demands.

In my current input column, I had my massage and acupuncture treatments. I also wanted to gradually increase both Pilates and tennis to twice a week once again. Of course, it was essential to continue my solitary walks in nature and to maintain my home as a safe nest where I might continue to rest and recoup. Now that the weather had turned warm again, I once again committed to having as many meals as possible outside on our deck.

Every Mother's Day it is our tradition to buy several beautiful hanging flowering baskets and lots of plants to fill the boxes along the deck railing, making it a colorful and welcoming haven. This year our efforts pleased two Carolina Wrens who built a nest in one of the hanging baskets. It was fun to watch the parents constantly flitting back and forth, first with nesting materials and then eventually with food for the open mouths of two begging chicks. Though these birds are very small, they have a very, loud song. "Teakettle, Teakettle, Teakettle!" Happily, this tune became my morning alarm clock.

Another family tradition is to host a large potluck cookout every Fourth of July. We live in the perfect location, an easy walking distance from the local fireworks. This cookout had become a tradition for many families whose children had grown up coming to this yearly event, some of whom were now bringing their own children. We could easily have seventy-five to one hundred people showing up. It required a remarkable amount of effort, spanning two weeks from planning, to set-up, to the actual event, followed by clean-up and several days' recuperation. It was always a wonderful celebration, but even though my family and friends all chipped in to help, I found it tremendously exhausting. I was dreading the thought of having it this particular year, but really struggling with the idea of canceling it. I hated the idea of disappointing so many people.

Another important lesson that I learned from Cheryl Richardson's *The Art of Extreme Self-Care:*

> *One of the harsh realities about practicing Extreme Self-Care is that you must learn to manage the anxiety that arises when other people are disappointed, angry, or hurt. And they will be. When you decide to break your patterns of self-sacrifice and deprivation, you'll need to start saying no, setting limits, and putting boundaries in place to protect your time, energy and emotional needs.*[18]

Despite having preached this reality in numerous women's group and retreats, I was having a hard time deciding what to do. "After all, I'm no longer really sick," I told myself. "My last chemo treatment was a month and a half ago." It was actually easier for me to think that we shouldn't have the cookout because it would disturb the little nest of wrens, than to admit it was too much for me. How ridiculous is that? Of course my family thought it was a foregone conclusion that we would be skipping the cookout this year, and obviously all the guests totally understood.

The Carolina Wren is unusual in that it sings loud and strong throughout the year, not just during the mating season like most songbirds. This family of wrens was encouraging me to let my voice resonate strongly throughout all my inner seasons. Who knew? Perhaps, learning to express my needs might serve as an inspiration for someone else as well. With this lesson in mind, I actually decided that it was time to put this tradition entirely to rest and only have smaller, more relaxing gatherings moving forward. My newfound ability to mindfully and graciously say "No" imparted a true sense of independence, freedom to follow my heart and sing my song.

---

[18]   Cheryl Richardson, *The Art of Extreme Self-Care: Transform Your Life One Month at a Time,* (California, Hay House 2009) p. 16

Turning

For everything there is a season, and
a time for every matter under heaven:
a time to be born, and a time to die;
a time to plant, and a time to pluck up
what is planted;
a time to kill, and a time to heal;
a time to break down, and a time to
build up;
a time to weep, and a time to laugh;
a time to mourn, and a time to dance.
~ The Holy Bible (KJV) Ecclesiastes 3:1-4

The seasons keep on turning, and most major transitions require more than one tour through their cycle. Initially, the journey requires a long *Winter* for both emotional and physical healing, but the insights revealed during that dark night of the soul remain with us. We become better equipped to weather the storms that lie ahead and to ride the winds of eternal change. The sequential cycles of a transition can fly by with milder *Winters*, quickly followed by brilliant *Springs* that flow gently into satisfying *Summers*.

Happy Anniversary

Whiskered Tern by Adrian Binns

This life is yours.
Take the power to choose what you want to do and do it well.
Take the power to love what you want in life and love it honestly.
Take the power to walk in the forest and be a part of nature.
Take the power to control your own life.
No one else can do it for you.
Take the power to make your life happy.

~ Susan Polis Schutz[21]

Synchronicity is a wondrous thing. Carol McClelland and I were preparing a new training program for coaches and therapists, *Unlocking Transition Anniversaries for Growth and Healing.* We chose September 11th to launch the program, for obvious reasons. I printed out the material and took it with me to proofread during my third maintenance treatment.

As I was reading through it I realized, "Wait! This month is the one-year anniversary of my initial diagnosis!" Even though I hadn't been consciously aware of this fact, my body remembered it. As we had been turning into the hospital drive, a deep feeling of dread had suddenly washed through me. I had wondered what that was about; these treatments weren't difficult. Now I understood: I was experiencing an anniversary reaction, reliving the moment when Carl drove me for my first chemo treatment.

Throughout the previous week, I had kept telling Carl, "I feel really anxious today and don't know why." I was also having a tough time managing all the details involved in returning to a full September teaching load. In retrospect, I see that these were also a part of my anniversary reaction, the clue being that I could not attribute any of my feelings to issues at hand.

Some psychologists believe that we experience anniversary reactions in order to process feelings that we were not able to deal with at the time of the event. One year previously, when I first received my diagnosis, I was overwhelmed with emotions and ignorant of what was to come. Now as I relived that period, I could confront and thereby release the dread that had been locked deep within my body. I was finally able to let the fear rise and then dissipate.

---

[21]   Susan Polis Schutz, *Yours If You Ask,* Continental Publication 1979, reprinted by permission. All rights reserved.

It became clear that this anniversary was another milestone that deserved commemoration. A year before, I had run to Cape May to await my fate alone. This time, contrary to my old pattern of solitary stoicism, I wanted to return with Carl to reward us both for having lived through a maelstrom of difficulties together.

My surprise anniversary present was the unexpected arrival of a foreign visitor, the Whiskered Tern. A native of Eastern Europe, this bird normally would have been migrating to Africa around now, but somehow it had been caught up in a current that blew it clear across the Atlantic. This was only the third time one had ever been spotted in the United States! Birders were arriving from all over the country to catch a glimpse. This small lost bird, a plain unremarkable creature in its homeland, was now infamous in America. It was destined to live out its life in a totally new frontier, hopefully to find a welcoming new community among the local terns and to join them on their migration south.

Who knows where the winds of change may take us? Or what the effect of our appearance in unknown territories might be? I do know that I would be content if my life brought as much excitement and joy to the world as this humble little tern.

Other anniversaries came and went. I completed my first year of maintenance treatments with just another year to go. Throughout the interminable long hours in the cancer center, a tee shirt had hung on the wall in direct view from my favorite chair. Now I was finally able fully appreciate its message:

Cancerican, Cerinoun: We define cancer as: the strength of resolve, the unifying of families and friends, and a new perspective on life.

The balance of my life/work/home was now intensely focused on living life fully. I decided to take another year's sabbatical from leading retreats and instead continue personal retreats and travels with the family. Carl and I went on another amazing trip with *Wildside Tours*, this time to the rainforests of Belize. While trekking through the jungle on the hunt for exotic birds, we spotted jaguar footprints in the mud. My wild soul soared. The joy of life rushed through my veins. *Spring* has sprung anew.

About the Author

Karin at World's End, by Carl Marcus

Karin Marcus is a Professional Life Coach and Master Retreat Leader in the Greater Philadelphia area. Her personal coaching style combines her love of the outdoors and respect for the human spirit. Karin's goal is to help everyone become an environmentalist of the heart. Her private practice, *Stepping Out Coaching*, focuses on supporting individuals through life's many transitions by helping them to embrace change and reinvent their lives. www.SteppingOutCoaching.com.

Karin has a B.S. in Physical Education and a M.A. in Movement Therapy. For twenty years she was the managing editor of The Fellowship Press, publishing the works of the Sufi teacher, M.R. Bawa Muhaiyaddeen. She is a Professional Certified Coach with the International Coaching Federation, a Board Certified Coach with the Center for Credentialing and Education, and a faculty member of The Institute for Life Coach Training. In addition, she is a Master Trainer for the *Seasons of Change®*.

Happily married for forty years, with their two grown daughters now living on their own, Karin and her husband Carl have more time to enjoy their passion for bird watching.

About the Photographers

Kitty Riley Kono is a self-taught photographer and naturalist, who operates her camera with the same love for observing and capturing wildlife as John James Audubon, demonstrating the same passion for beauty, composition and light.

When she retired in 2007, after serving 32 years in the non-profit world, her husband and daughter gave her a Nikon digital camera, and her love of nature and photography blossomed first in Japan, where she spent a year photographing landscapes and wildlife, and then in Valley Forge National Park when she returned to the United States.

She has published seven books of nature photography, the latest being *Tanzania*. She lives with her husband, daughter, and cat in St. Davids, Pennsylvania.

Adrian Binns, a naturalist and amateur field ornithologist, grew up in Morocco and England, where his birding experiences paved the way for a career in the birding community. As a tour guide, Adrian has led eco-tours for a variety of organizations and tour companies to 5 continents since the early 1990's and joined Wildside Nature Tours in 2007.

An accomplished avian illustrator and photographer, his images regularly appear in all the major birding magazines and media formats. In a 2006 issue, Wild Bird magazine named Adrian one of the "upcoming leaders to watch!" Adrian has worked with Birding Adventures TV on several episodes, including Hawk Mountain and Botswana.

Richard Crossley was born in Yorkshire, England. This internationally-acclaimed birder and photographer grew up living for sport. Already hooked on birding at age seven, he hitchhiked over 100,000 miles to follow his passion. In his twenties, he traveled more extensively, particularly to Asia and North America. He fell in love with Cape May, NJ, and he has lived there since 1991.

Self-employed in corporate America, in recent times he has turned his attention to books and the role of photography. Since *The Shorebird Guide,* Richard's goal has been to make lifelike scenes that are more visually striking and educational. With multiple projects on the go, Crossley Books and *The Crossley ID Guide* series are intended to have a significant impact on how we look at birds, wildlife, and books.

Carl Marcus is a psychotherapist, amateur photographer, Sufi student, bird watcher, and companion extraordinaire.

The Coaches

Helene Van Manen, MCC specializes in training Coaches to lead retreats and is the founder and director of Retreat Coaches—the premier training institute for wo(men) wishing to lead retreats. She has trained hundreds of women to lead retreats and as a result, Retreat Coaches are reaching groups all over the globe through her leadership. Currently she is also on the Faculty of Coach U and is a Professional Mentor Coach who works with new Coaches in Training. **http://www. retreatcoaches.com/**

Valerie Brown is a Courage & Renewal® Facilitator prepared by the Center forCourage & Renewal. A consultant and principal of Lead Smart Coaching, LLC, specializing in leadership and mindfulness training. For more information about Valerie and her work: **http://www.leadsmartcoaching.com/**

Carol Kortsch was born in Africa, raised and educated in Canada, and now lives, works, and writes from Stonehaven Commons in Radnor, PA. She is a facilitator prepared by the Center for Courage & Renewal and offers retreats from her wilderness soul as a life adventurer and Earth listener. **http://www.*stonehavencommons.org***

Julie Schelling, ACC is a work/life renewal coach and founder of Coaching for Resonance. She specializes in stress management, using mindfulness practices. She is the author of *Invitation to Believe,* a book based on her spiritual journey to find the purpose of life. For more information visit: **http://www.coachingforresonance.com.**

About the Seasons of Change®

The *Seasons of Change* model provides insights for those in transition, whether they entered their transition by choice or by circumstance, whether the transition was anticipated or came as a complete surprise.

The *Seasons of Change* offers a multi-faceted, nature-based metaphor in a natural way in order to approach life changes. Nature has developed a wide range of responses to the ever-changing seasons. These responses provide a rich foundation of knowledge, inspiration, hope, and direction to those in transition.

Each season (or phase) of the transition process has its own signs, actions, and detours. This information gives you a map to follow as you navigate your own transition. The visually memorable nature metaphors associated with each season are simple, powerful tools that provide constant support and guidance through difficult times.

To read more about the *Seasons of Change* metaphor:
http://www.seasonsofchange.com/seasons-of-change.html

To learn about upcoming *Seasons of Change* trainings, for coaches, counselors, therapists and other professionals who support clients in transition: http://www.seasonsofchange.com/seasons-of-change-training-for-professionals.html

To find a *Seasons of Change* coach:
http://www.seasonsofchange.com/find-a-seasons-of-change-coach.html

CPSIA information can be obtained at www.ICGtesting.com
Printed in the USA
BVOW05s2001040816

457742BV00007B/5/P

9 781504 356541